To Barbara
Best wishes
Frances.

HAND LUGGAGE ONLY

The shortlist anthology of Open Poetry's
2007 International Sonnet Competition

edited with an introduction
by Christopher Whitby

OPEN POETRY LTD

First published in Great Britain 2008
by
Open Poetry Ltd
Island House
Arthur Street
Barwell
Leicestershire LE9 8AH

www.openpoetry.org.uk

ISBN: 978-0-9559162-0-5

Designed by Dragonfly Presentation Graphics Ltd
www.dragonflypg.co.uk

Printed by Biddles Limited
24 Rollesby Road, Hardwick Industrial Estate,
King's Lynn, Norfolk PE30 4LS

CONTENTS

INTRODUCTION

I

This anthology contains the 100 sonnets shortlisted for the final round of judging in Open Poetry's inaugural International Sonnet Competition in 2007.

The judges were Susan Bassnett, Jacqueline Osherow and Don Paterson, to whom I would like to record my thanks for agreeing to undertake that role. 1,978 competition entries were received, which were whittled down to the 100 sonnets in this anthology for selection of the winners. That a few poets achieved two sonnets in the shortlist is not entirely surprising. The poems were judged with complete author anonymity, but the work of a good poet will usually show consistent quality across multiple competition entries.

All shortlisted sonnets are published here in alphabetical order of poets' names, but on pages xix-xxiv you will find details of the top 3 prizewinners and the 3 highly commended entries together with comments by the judges. Short biographies of each poet are at the end of the book.

It is just possible that you may have seen one or two of the sonnets in this anthology, or versions of them, before. How could they been allowed into the competition? Occasionally a poet will win a prize for his or her work or get paid by a magazine or book publisher. For most of the time, however, acceptance of a poet's work for publication in the media brings no reward other than the publicity itself and the poet is in essence subsidising the media rather than vice versa. It was a conscious decision in formulating the competition rules not to bar sonnets that had been previously published or appeared on a poet's or an independent website, providing that *no remuneration* (excluding any complimentary copy of a journal or similar) had been received.

It remains something of an unfortunate imbalance that the same poem or collection, once published, can receive more than one major prize (e.g. Forward and T. S. Eliot prizes) and yet competitions usually forbid entry of any poem which has been 'published' in any way, including these days on a poet's personal website, which in some cases may receive few visitors beyond friends and family and the serendipity visitor whose cat has, with curious intelligence, walked across the keyboard. Before the advent of desktop publishing and the internet, 'publication' was relatively easy to define; now it is rather more contentious. Eric Blomquist's *Sonnet Board* website (www.sonnets.org), which can be accessed by anyone although only members can post comments, recently contained some discussion as to whether posting a sonnet for workshop comment and review could be construed as publication. The members decided it should not, but it is conceivable that some competition organisers might disagree.

Workshopping poems on bulletin boards also raises the question as to whether a later revised version of a poem constitutes a new poem or not with respect to any definition of its having already been published. We all know that our revisions sometimes just tighten up a poem and sometimes alter its tenor altogether. Who is to arbitrate here?

One major problem with competitions is that they tend to regard themselves as exclusive in the sense that poets usually get no guidance from the organisers in deciding whether it is permissible to enter the same poem in more than one competition. What if an entry wins a place in one competition while another in which it is entered has not yet got to the stage of final judgement? Open Poetry's Sonnet Competition had to face that one, when an entrant with admirable honesty advised that his sonnet had received a modestly remunerative placing in another competition before ours had closed. Making an off-the-cuff judgement, I responded that the entrant could either offer an alternative or, since *at the time of entry* the poem had received no remuneration, we would be happy for it to remain in the competition and ignore its interim success.

While I am all for encouraging new poetry, competitions are not themselves the main instigators of poets continuing to add to their body of work and competition organisers at least *appear* to be unmindful of the fact that when a poem is entered into a competition, the 'unpublished' rule immediately consigns that poem to a limbo existence whereby the poet can do very little else with it until the competition results are announced. I wonder just how many good poems are locked away from public view for long periods simply because they are awaiting judgement in this way.

And here's a small thought for the future. Passing poems around friends by email may be considered the equivalent of circulating them in manuscript, but suppose a poem is the subject of a 'viral campaign'. This is similar to those nuggets of wisdom or humour you receive by email forwarded by someone you know but originally instigated by someone you don't, arriving with you only after being forwarded through a host of people with whom you have no immediate connection. It is in essence the spread of information by the electronic equivalent of word of mouth, but it is perhaps also definable as a form of publication. A 'no remuneration' rule can easily cater for this; an 'unpublished' rule faces difficulty.

Not all readers will agree that every poem in this book is really a sonnet, but one of the aims of the competition was to allow room for experimentation. It was never the intention simply to find the best imitation of a sonnet from a past age, the equivalent of reproduction furniture. The sonnet has developed over time, not in the sense that innovations have consigned earlier manifestations to the wastebin, but rather that new shoots have grown on the solid trunk of tradition. All the great Renaissance practitioners, not least that arch experimenter Sir Philip Sidney, were incorporating innovations of form and subject into their sonnets and what we now regard as 'traditional' was exciting new territory for them. The history of the sonnet is a history of development as much as of conformance. The sonnet is a tough old bird and can survive a lot of pulling about without dropping down dead.

The proof of this is that no two people seem to agree what makes a sonnet. Some have very rigid criteria, insisting on iambic pentameters and only rhyme schemes that have settled into being 'traditional'; others disagree, sometimes violently. I will not attempt to better the reasoning of Don Paterson in his introduction to *101 Sonnets* (Faber) to explain why that volume contains sonnets that a number of readers will dismiss as just 14 line poems, but I would add the following argument in relation to one 'rule' that some consider essential for a poem to be a true sonnet – the use of iambic pentameters.

The iambic pentameter is very common in English sonnets, but not in those of other languages and cultures. Petrarch did not use them for a start. One reason why they are almost universal in the first flowering of the sonnet in England during the Renaissance is simply that the iambic pentameter was one of the most common measures used in *all* English poetry at that time, and as it happens also on the stage. It was ubiquitous.

The commonest poetic form today is free verse, quite often using lines much less than ten syllables in length, irrespective of any persistent rhythm. So why should *our* commonest contemporary verse form be incapable of use in a sonnet? The parity with Renaissance sonnet structure is not then the iambic pentameter itself, but the use of the prevailing verse form of the time. Thus if an entry to the competition was in short-line free verse form (but still within the simple 14 line rule we set) and had the *feel* of a sonnet, because within that free form it exhibited a number of other characteristics that just spoke 'sonnet', then it was deemed worthy of consideration for the shortlist and final round of judging.

It is also worth remembering that the person who defined the curtal sonnets of Gerard Manley Hopkins as being 'real' sonnets was none other than Gerard Manley Hopkins – a prime example of self-certification. To nail the definition of a sonnet down to compliance with all the 'rules' that anyone has ever thought of as imperative for the form would be to secure the sonnet into a coffin. I am more of the mind that we should listen to that great twentieth century icon, Mr Spock, as he passes his life-form sensor over the body of a poem and declares: "It's a sonnet, Jim, but not as we know it."

If we could all agree just what a sonnet is, it would be a piece of dead meat. It lives because we can't agree on it. Apart from that, before we can define a sonnet for all eternity, we need to consider whether any particular example of the form even qualifies as poetry. So the first question then is: 'what is poetry?' At this point I pass you the baton...

* * * * * * *

II

Anatomy of a Competition
for anyone who wonders what goes on

The origins of Open Poetry's inaugural International Sonnet Competition lie essentially in frustration. When I returned to writing poetry in later life, having (I hoped) left self-conscious outpourings far behind, I very quickly had a modest success with a sonnet in a BBC Radio 4 competition that for practical reasons limited the poem length to no more than 14 lines.*

Having rediscovered an affinity with the sonnet, I found myself using the form more and more often, delighting in its unexpected ability to tackle any subject and embrace an extraordinary number of variations on its apparent 'set rules' and especially in its power to focus the mind, both of the writer and the reader. In short I found it liberating, in contrast to free verse which shackled me with two much possibility and not enough inevitability. I must confess that I maintain a view that much free verse would benefit from being distilled down to half its length.

To attribute the famine that followed my first success to anything other than my submissions not being good enough would be foolish, but I did begin to notice that it was rare indeed for a sonnet to appear in the shortlist of any competition with a major prize. There are a number of small sonnet competitions that surface periodically, but they do not offer significant prizes, giving the impression that the sonnet is something of a backwater.

The only major sonnet competition seemed to be the Nemerov, but as that will not accept online submissions and requires the entry fee to be paid in US dollars, drawn on a US bank to boot, it is essentially an American affair. Anyone who has needed to pay for something in a currency other than their own knows how easy that is online and how time-

---

* Second prize, being some volumes of poetry, was an infinitely preferable result to winning first prize, which was a sculpture on the theme of *Arrival and Departure*. Since it was a radio competition, just what this sculpture looked like remains a mystery to this day. If that 1991 winner happens to pick up this volume, may I ask if you were pleased with your prize?

consuming and expensive it is by bank draft or other paper means.

The rarity of sonnets appearing in major competition shortlists seemed a little odd in the light of the number of contemporary sonnets that are written and indeed published. Although they must be heavily outnumbered in volume by other forms, especially free verse, are they equally outgunned in terms of poetic craft?

As a form, the sonnet transcends borders, being popular in most European languages, and an internet search even turned up an article entitle *The Modern Chinese Sonnet* – though it did not state whether these are in 14 columns! So why were they so absent from competition shortlists, especially when rightly or wrongly one can start imagining that one can identify a 'type' of free verse that keeps reappearing in the shortlists?*

Whatever the reason, there seemed to be a gap waiting to be filled that would enable poets worldwide to submit their sonnets to a dedicated competition both by post and online, without currency issues, and with a substantial amount of prize money. The journey to bring this idea into being was instructive, sometimes entertaining, and generally far more labour-intensive that I had imagined. Still, as the inventor Daniel Doyce says in Dickens' *Little Dorritt*:

> *You hold your life on the condition that to the last*
> *you shall struggle hard for it. Every man holds a*
> *discovery on the same terms.*

So too for an idea.

The first question was where the prize money was going to come from. Most major competitions have sponsors (arts bodies, generous businesses, media companies), but without a track record to place in front of potential sponsors it was soon evident that the competition would have to be self-funding,

---

* This may be a controversial view, but it has not been dispelled for me by my doing well in a competition with a block of poems that included a free verse offering taken from a bottom drawer and dusted off because I thought it looked like 'a competition poem'. Of the submitted poems selected for the subsequent competition anthology, this one was amongst those published. I didn't like it then and I don't like it now, but it did *so* look like a competition archetype, as perhaps events proved.

with any shortfall being underwritten personally. That should have been the time to back away from the idea, but I referred back to Daniel Doyce. The number of entries the competition would receive was an unknown and so where to pitch the entry fee was equally in doubt, with all the added uncertainty of how the level of entry fee would affect the number of entries.

A draft business plan, including estimates of expected costs, especially for marketing and publicity, was, like all business plans, largely a work of fiction, but in the end an entry fee was fixed but with a bonus to mitigate the expense that every third sonnet entered in a block would be free. Bearing in mind that online entries always lost to Paypal a commission percentage, a fixed transaction fee and for overseas entries a currency conversion fee as well, a non-UK entry of 3 sonnets (including the free one) would actually only contribute 63% of the single entry fee per poem into the competition pot – maybe more than sufficient for a subsidised competition, but not ideal for one that has to fund itself. Foreseeing the revenue was therefore very much a mix of intuition and of guesswork.

The next question was how to find the judges, Fortunately internet searching soon turned up contact details of poets or their agents and email requests proved relatively fast, despite having to wait to hear back from a potential judge before moving on to ask another. It was an early decision to have 3 judges rather than one, as that is what the most prestigious competitions do. There would therefore be 3 fees to find, and although that meant more expense, as the self-employed husband of a professional musician I am all too aware that professionals need to be paid realistically for their time. In his novel *Soul Music* Terry Pratchett summed up what every professional musician wants to hear in the words: "I enjoyed that. Here's some money. When can I hear you again?" The first and last sentences are merely feeding vanity and not the family without the middle one being present. Too much of the world thinks that art should be pursued only for love, not money; the bill from a musician or writer is somehow a surprise in the way that a bill from an accountant or lawyer is not.

Then came concerns about transparency. If you take people's money for any reason, they have a right to know how it's being spent. I find it odd that it is not easy to get hold of the separate accounts of most poetry competitions, so it is very hard to find any paradigm to work to. For reasons of openness, I decided to run the competition through a limited company, so that the accounts would always be available through UK Companies House. That they are also now published on the competition website is not a legal requirement, but something I instinctively felt should be done. Open Poetry Ltd was incorporated in the full knowledge that there would be higher accountancy costs, but I felt that was indubitably better than running the competition as a personal affair and using a 'trading as' bank account.

The next step was to decide the rules and build the website for online entries. At least I had the skills to do the latter myself, rather than having to pay someone else, so if the competition ended up requiring subsidy, the website work would not be one of the expenses to meet.

But the rules... ah, the rules. Independently of Don Paterson's arguments in his introduction to *101 Sonnets* that I have referred to earlier, I also arrived at a simple 14 line rule with all other aspects of the form being open to challenge. It was a practical solution on the grounds that we had a simply understood condition for entry (although counting the lines proved too difficult for a very small number of entrants!) and that 14 liners would make themselves felt as sonnets or not as the case might be. To ensure parity, the website and leaflet made it clear that the competition would treat traditional/ formal sonnets and freeform/innovatory sonnets on an equal basis. Whatever the structural form, the quality of the sonnet as poetry would be paramount and poetry is more than either form or content in themselves.

The 14 line rule caused a few complaints of course. Why no curtal sonnets? Caudate sonnets? What about drop line sonnets? – which is like asking 'when is a line not a line?' *Whitby's Rule* now states that even if you set a group of people only one very simple and clear rule to which they must adhere, they will still seek to bend it – though come to think of it, perhaps that should be called *The Eden Rule*.

So the competition ran, and by and large in a fairly untroubled way, though I did begin to wilt at times under the weight of preparing texts, so we had copies with and without contact details of the poets, all referenced by a unique tracking number. In future I will automate some of the duplication tasks for online entries by adding extra functions to the webform coding.

Online payments via Paypal caused problems for a very small number of entrants, although this was on some occasions simply because they already had Paypal accounts they had forgotten about. There were occasional other difficulties that I never got to the bottom of, although sending a Paypal 'money request' by email seemed to be a solution that worked every time. Incidentally Paypal was not the first choice for the transactions but a major UK bank looked at the competition and declined to offer facilities because in their book – and they always go by the tick boxes in their books – it was 'too much like gambling'! No skill involved in poetry then?

The countries where we had to use circuitous routes were Myanmar and Lebanon: Myanmar has no credit card system and Lebanon is not on Paypal's acceptance list. Solutions were found. Not so for the three phone calls I fielded from Nigeria where well-spoken enquirers asked for bank account details so they could transfer the entry fee direct into the account – for 'my client' in one case. Yesterday was I not born.

Yet even as late as September 2007, nine months after launch, the competition was far from being in the black. Then October happened. Entries flooded in at a pace that I could barely keep up with and the goal of self-funding was achieved.

In the end my role was always that of a facilitator. It is the poets who have made the competition a success, who have made it 'work', and who have announced very loudly that sonnet writing is alive and well and living all over the world. I hope you enjoy this anthology.

Christopher Whitby
Open Poetry Ltd

First Prize

Julie Kane – 'Used Book'
[see page 46]

Judges' comments:

'Used Book' does what most poems would like to do, but usually fail to: it finds itself happy enough in its form to wholly transcend its form, and the reader ends up too lost in the spell of the poem to notice the fine technique that's casting the spell in the first place. It's only afterwards – after being entertained and charmed and moved – that you realize what a fine sonnet this is. The English sonnet can often stumble in its closing couplet; too often, it's used to provide a redundant summary, a 'moral', or a neat ending the poem might have been better without. No chance of that here: the poet waits until the last two lines to time the poem's miserable epiphany. Elsewhere there's so much to admire, so many expert touches: the powerful sound-sense of 'with one whole wall'; the deadly timing of that 'out of luck'; the way the metre is used to enforce the correct stressing of 'Jarrell'; the Frostian leisure of the parenthesis, 'all in all'; the way the speaker's excitement is communicated in that rushed enjambment 'familiar backbone of ...' But most impressive is the poem's unity, achieved through the poet's ruthless marshalling of the material. No detail, however apparently casual or arbitrary, fails to advance the plot. The poem's easy confidence disguises a brutal concentration and focus that puts you in mind of that early 20th century master, Edwin Arlington Robinson – which is as high praise as you could give a sonneteer.

Second Prize

Daniel Neumann – 'Two Moments'
[see page 63]

Judges' comments:

This is a very well-crafted sonnet. It uses the classic English variant of the sonnet form, three sets of four line rhymes and a final couplet, that is so often a vehicle for irony or a sudden change of mood. 'Two Moments' is remarkable for its understatement in its exploration of the complexity and endurance of unconsummated love as well as the lasting power of a seemingly small gesture. It says a great deal about the often indirect nature of emotional communication. Particularly striking is the contrast between the speaker's approach and the approach of the person whose gesture the speaker is recounting. The writer uses very direct, clear, no-nonsense language to convey the profundity of what can't be spoken directly. How ingenious to make the turn in this sonnet not a change in point of view or circumstance or opinion, but rather an obstinate permanence; an ironic twist in the narrative, when the unidentified recipient of the man's gift meets his wife. The sonnet packs a great deal into its fourteen lines, there is a novel struggling to be released here, and the simplicity of the language and the rhyme scheme are underpinned by a complex weaving of the story line. The writer's ability to condense so much into the space allowed is impressive.

Third Prize

Alison Mace – 'Wartime Picnic'
[see page 53]

Judges' comments:

It is the rare that any poem, let alone a sonnet, manages to encapsulate both a moment and a lifetime to convey the profound personal repercussions of momentous historical or political events. 'Wartime Picnic' does all this with quiet grace; taking on enormous subjects through a detailed exploration of a child's perfect afternoon. It explores not only the high adult costs of charmed childhood memories, and the hardship of war on those at home, but the long-lasting negative and embittering effects of wartime death. Especially impressive is the way the poet uses the poetic convention of the sonnet's turn to convey a cataclysmic and permanent life change.

THE WINNERS

Highly Commended

John Haynes – 'First Thing'
[see page 42]

Judges' comments:

'First Thing' is a fine Miltonic sonnet written in a single sentence, and maps its syntax to the flow of the poet's thought in a wholly convincing way. The delicate use of half-rhyme and the quietly varied *caesurae* give the impression of a lovely conversational ease, and it's only later that you notice the great skill with which it's all been put together. It also shows how we can overrate 'subject matter': all the poetry here is in the telling, and in the originality of the poet's approach.

Lydia Macpherson – 'Lessons'
[see page 55]

Judges' comments:

'Lessons' is a disturbing sonnet that inverts the traditional use of the form to express love. The language recalls Elizabeth Barrett Browning, but the subject – domestic violence – challenges the very nature of the love poem. The bitterly ironic voice is consistent, the juxtapositioning of words of ensnarement with images of brutality that is evident in the opening line is developed through the careful patterns of rhyme through to the final shocking sentence. A well-written, powerful and moving sonnet that leaves a lasting impression.

Highly Commended

William Orem – 'Crucifix, Church of the Most Blessed Sacrament, Washington, D.C'
[see page 66]

Judges' comments:

'Crucifix, Church of the Most Blessed Sacrament' is a well-controlled poem full of sharp observation, fine original phrasemaking, and real feeling. The naturalness of the turn reminds us how the sonnet – at least when it's used with this sensitivity and expertise – is a form perfectly fitted to a certain turn of human thought. There's evidence of a fine ear at work here, and almost every line seems to have a distinct consonantal signature.

JUDGES' GENERAL COMMENTS

Judging this competition has been a fascinating experience. The sonnet form is still one to which writers are drawn, perhaps because the fourteen line framework offers particular challenges. It is a very condensed form of poetry, yet in its tightness there is always the possibility of ideas and images exploding outwards towards the reader.'

Susan Bassnett

What a joy to know that so many people are still writing sonnets in English; these entries demonstrate the sonnet's flexibility and versatility as well as its stamina. It was a pleasure to read them.'

Jacqueline Osherow

Overall the standard was pleasingly high, and there were many poems in the final 100 which demonstrated considerable skill with the form. Most had to be discounted for failing to honour the unity of theme that the sonnet insists upon, and contained too many different elements to be united in the poem's short span: if nothing else, sonnet-writing is a crash course in wielding Occam's razor. However the winners all displayed the necessary discipline and concentration, and in every case I was too moved or interested to notice or care whether they were sonnets or not: this, for me, is a sign of real expertise. Other judges on another day might have placed them in a different order – but I'm convinced these six fine poems would have found themselves on anyone's shortlist.

Don Paterson

HAND LUGGAGE ONLY

MIKE ALEXANDER

The Sirens' Answer

You filled your ears with sealing wax, sailed
within an inch of transcendental song,
a glory coveted as one among
the numbered wonders of the sea: fish-tailed,

we bared our human breasts as we regaled
your vessel with our singing, singing long
through your prosaic skulls. You did us wrong
to claim in your accounts our shanties failed.

Although you dulled our melodies to keep
what arguments you treasured most intact,
our musicking is subtler & deep

enough to wash away the dregs of fact —
we sing your darkest voyage as you sleep,
until you wake, eyes leaking, voices cracked.

One-Way Ticket

They closed the line and just the track remains.
The miners' railway where we used to play
in far-off summers, when I came to stay,
echoes with the ghosts of long-gone trains.

Cwm Cynfal and the Ceunant ring with wild
unchanging songs of childhood. Years away
mean nothing there. When I returned today
they called to me, and knew me as their child.

The rest is altered irretrievably.
My kin died years ago or else moved on:
no point in staying once the work was gone.
How few there are who still remember me.

My ties are broken far beyond repair:
the line is closed and just the tracks are there.

*Cwm Cynfal and the Ceunant: the valley and gorge of the River
Cynfal in Wales*

Water Bearer

Each dawn, before the sun devoured the shade
and seared the arid land, a potter strode
down to the well along a dusty road
to fill a well-used water jar he'd made.

As he returned one day a stranger said,
"Your jar is fractured. Anyone can see
you waste your time and labour fruitlessly.
The water spills along the track you tread."

The potter answered, "Though it leaks it still
retains enough for me, and I would not,
for all its flaws, discard my battered pot.
It has a further purpose to fulfil."

Where he had passed a radiant display
of flowers bobbed to greet the breaking day.

Bluebelling

Up Eileen Gardens, down Cooks Lane, we called
for friends with jam sandwiches and warm pop,
passing lawns crowded by daffodils, and
tulips neat and sweet as scoops of rainbow
kali. Spring-sap summoned us, Robin's men,
and every girl Maid Marion. Beguiled
by a green man, a lad in the lane, we
plunged into the old wood laughing, laughing.

We knew where to find the blue of thunder
and damp mornings; the blue of lilac, mauve
and indigo; the blue with a scent that
teased as we eased it from slippery stems.

Up Cooks Lane, down Eileen Gardens, we came
home; arms aching with drooping sheaves of blue.

The Statue of Snow (1494)

Snow swirled down across the slow grey Arno,
blanketing the city, stifling its stench,
drifted through arches to soften the square
stone palazzo where a sculptor carved, teased,
and half-released from transient crystals:
muscles, ribs, sinews, veins, an angel's face
and genitals of ice so true, boys squealed
and mothers covered the eyes of daughters.

Michaelangelo fulfilled his duty;
Piero de' Medici was content.
Ruler and city were both glorified
by a statue soon stolen by the thaw.

But whores coiling coppery hair still pause,
to dream of a man awakened from snow.

Tree Dreams

If she holds her twig-brittle finger bones tight
in a fist, her knuckle bones rise up white;
stub-buds of new limbs, pressing her skin.

They hover close, under the surface, wait
for a signal, trigger. They itch for the light
and to move in it, grow to it, drink it all in.

They're greedy. She glimpses their dreams some nights,
dreams of branches, galaxies wide,
of fruit like planets, seeds like suns.

She frisks herself for gnarls and twists,
reads each bone-knot as a sign, it's time
to change, the spring has come;

they shoot from her like splinters, scythes,
leave her skin-split like a pip and rise rise rise

When Daddy Comes Home

There is a moment in our day – which hitherto
had teemed with dimpled laughter,
tumbled, nudged and winked its way
across the sunlit birdsong-speckled hours –
there is a moment when the quivering springness
starts to slow; an instant when the light falls wingless
to the cold earth, a sudden folding of the flowers,
a hush of footfall poised upon the roaring brink
where, with buckled breath, we wait – we wait for you…

Push your joy into dark corners, make yourself small,
squeeze your mirth into a tight little ball,
press your shadow up against the wall
then close your eyes.

He may not even notice you at all.

Killing the Beast

To honour the beast I looked in his eyes,
my knee to his throat, his horn in my fist,
hoping for peace in his luminous gaze,
an aye from his eye, foretaste of the bliss
awaiting us once haruspical rites
were duly fulfilled – brute complicity
in the unerring truth of priest and knife,
the heave of his throat offered willingly.

Wild mirrors his eyes, reflecting the blade,
bright flash of silver in fathomless wells,
no bovine blessing but a thrashing rage,
then the stab of loss as the sharp edge fell
and in his passing, a vision revealed
of dew licked from grass in green morning fields.

Hormones & Harry James

Retreat from the second-floor marriage bed
no option once they found privacy there,
found his virgin fingers worked her virgin

locks, her mother's bass snores from the extra
upstairs bedroom no deterrent to first
base, second, third, or going all the way–

hormones & Harry James records perfect
harmony in that cold December of
'44. Kept from war by a crippled

left arm (he was stillborn & the doctor
ripped him out arm first), he was man enough
for this homefront campaign, potent enough

for a first-time father, lucky enough
her Doughboy dad didn't own a shotgun.

(Part of a sequence)

Fate Is Larger

The kids would marry with blessings in June,
just past her graduation. The boy could
find some job somewhere, dropping-out was no

sin, particularly with his discipline
problem. Never mind that he rebelled 'cause
he was smarter than most, & bored with dull

pedantry passing for education;
that his painter's eye & verbal wit set
him well above the scrabbling neighborhood

norm; the moral weight of his one mistake
would shape him now, as Maine had shaped his new
father-in-law, glacially grind fun from

his life, color from his painter's palette,
teach him fate is larger than his designs.

(Part of a sequence)

Snowman

It's two years now since we last met.
Your messages breach ex-textiquette.
You jest of testing my new bed.
Your thumb revives jokes long since dead.
Your virtual flirting (i'm on the train!)
becomes 'can i c u again?'

Pint to pint, brushing knees in the crowded room,
you falter and say – *the wedding's in June.*

All at once, like falling, I remember
you rolling an enormous snowman in a blizzard
for me. Us two, the Downs, that December.
You marked with sodden wool-gloved hand the word

Love. Nose dripping above, throwing me that same
                              sweet sidelong glance
you're giving me now I've missed my chance.

JOAN BENNER

Timescape

The scent of apples drifts like distant bells
on this the open day at the apple farm.
October's round again; the people come
with four-wheel drives and wellies through the fields
where hard-trod grass lays bare enduring soil.
Ripeness is now our measurement of time:
we're gatherers again; our instincts home
from ancestry passed far beyond recall.

Like ruddy lanterns lit by autumn sun
the pippins, pick-loose, dangle from the tree.
I think of bells swung out for death or birth,
and watch the children's reaching fingers learn
the fit of roundness. Not eternity,
but comfort of circles, seasons, apple earth.

Head of Christ on a Breadboard

In the shadows and reluctance of the shed,
Darkened by old acquaintance with rain,
The roof lifting, the roof-felt torn,
The slats rotten to the muscular thread
Of pushy brambles, thick with thorn,
Where the previous owner's wood was stored,
Spider-shrouded, I found a breadboard
That bore a recognisably human stain.

Perhaps the iconic resemblance was faint –
No match for the whole ebay Host
Of miraculous faces in pastries and toast –
But a spill of metallic-gold Airfix paint
Gave a Byzantine look to the Christ,
Criss-crossed, scored, endlessly sliced.

Colour Coordination

My father had a taste for black with brown:
they criss-crossed on his favourite slipover;
his slacks were soot or charcoal, breezing down
to meet his burnt-sienna shoes and cover
socks whose stripes went black brown black brown black.
My mother frowned. I can't recall him once
in blue and green (her biggest no-no). Back
in those cancelled days she also looked askance
at black with navy, brown with any blue.

I never learned what colour shoes would pass
with a navy suit. Who cares? You disapprove
of blue teamed up with green? To hell with you.
Tell that, one fine day, to the years-long grass
that covers their bones, and to the sky above.

Faith

Miss P. believes in fairies, whom she sees,
and in a God whom she has never seen.
The fairies pluck her like a violin.
God is a distant father, hard to please.

Sixty years ago she met a man
and took his Christian courtesy for love.
She made a dangerous pact with God above.
She kept the faith. The Almighty let her down.

She's lived her long life quietly doing good.
She tithes her pension. The vicar thinks she's fey.
He never hears the tune the fairies play.
He does not trespass on her solitude.

Three times each Sunday, and at midweek mass,
she still asks God for human love. Alas.

JOSEPHINE BROGAN

The Ode to Joy

On the balcony at St. Joseph's School,
looking down on the medal-winners boxed
behind the civic heads – my eldest scared,
her lanky sister amongst the band, bored, why on earth
has this to be endured – at last the moment
and the Ode to Joy is scraping off her cello string...

and the next thing, under my thighs
a Triumph bike guns; two shadows tilt,
going with the camber of the road; a moon climbs,
vineyards ahead. The spool unwinds a year, a river –
all really there ever was and here this pearl,
this perfectly smooth little world, drops
from its rosary. Home, I park it pillowdeep;
it clings. And seeds like crazy in the dark.

Missing the Point

The cream-flecked greening beauty of the sea,
incessant, ebbed and flowed across the sand,
rippling your toes, steadily rising. Bloody cold,
but you had a point to make, held your arm out boldly.
Now they'd see the limits of our human agency;
even a crown's powers are only finite,
never absolute. But can you teach
a lesson no-one really wants to hear?

I guess you must be well pissed off, your name
become a byword for arrogance,
and you a figure of fun. The roaring tide
of our avoidance is relentless, and no single hand
can halt the waters, swirling blind,
drowning the laughing land.

Gravity
with thanks to ML

The aerialist swings up and out, beyond
the proscenium arch. Collectively,
we gasp; she reaches the dead point of pure
weightlessness, lets go of the *corde volante*.
Arms outstretched, hair as wild as Medusa:
for less than a heartbeat she's still, born
above us by art and trust, untouched
by gravity, time. I have to choose –
do I imagine the slender, sweat-damp figure,
hair tied back, hands calloused and scarred,
stowing away the ropes and shackles
after the audience has gone? She fixes me
with tunnel eyes. *Whatever you want to think,*
she says, *I cannot fly. I fall professionally.*

BRENDA ANN BURKE

Passing It Forward

Not the girl this time, the boy. Bent over
a low table pulling from a sketch-pad
one clawed foot. A curved talon emerges,
stinking scales layered, oozing blood and charcoal.

Devil project is already past due.
But he, archaeologist at work, must
proceed carefully, unearthing the beast
square by square. Failed attempts litter the floor.

The world is so impatient. Kids attached
squirming to weekly schedules. I wonder
where this square peg will fit. Who looks after
the seers, unfashionably intense?

The creature burrows down further,
having no wish to be freed.

(Number 2 of a sequence of 2)

CHRISSIE BURY

Two Rooms

In that small room, a summary of life,
a snapshot of her few remaining years.
Across the too short space from bed to chairs,
memories of a mother, daughter, wife.
The home-made shelves of broken ornaments,
an ancient case of treasured, well-loved books,
favourite photos smiling down from hooks
and, on the window ledge, two wilting plants.
But in this room, there's nothing save her sighs
which fade away like flowers she cannot see,
and words we pour into the emptiness.
Beyond the endless days of last goodbyes,
of holding hands and whispering tenderly,
she'll slip like falling snow to quietness.

Nocturne

When we are done, you and I, and all this mess
of love and sweat is just a faded stain;
When loving hands instead of a caress
reach for the evening paper with disdain;
What will we say, you and I, when the nest
has emptied and we have nothing to sustain
the nights when silence is the only guest?
Will we still, you and I, even try
to rekindle love, now in its last arrest?
Or will the final act be a lengthy sigh
of boredom too withering to bear?
When it comes to that, our last goodbye,
will we forget how much we once each cared?
Are we done, do you think, you and I?

John in the Kitchen, Reading

Expert in words, food and whistling
and all the vocabulary of kitchen:

the sturdy epic of casseroles,
epigrams of peppers and spices;

you know the long poem of the Welsh dresser
which is full of adjectives – too many, I would say.

On the window sill, a vernacular of milk jugs
and on the marble top, whole dialects of cheeses.

Now, the window tilts morning and clouds
are verbs, too irregular to memorise.

Other syntaxes persist in woks and saucepans
but the mirror conforms to the grammar of sunlight

and there's the noun of you – singular you –
centre stage, as complete as a sonnet.

Day In Day Out

I'd love to grab that grizzling mobile phone
And shriek into the frenzied chatterer's ear:
Why do you have to shout so we can hear?
I'd ditch his head piece; leaving him lying prone.

I dream of opening up that window wide
To let the train dust filter through my hair,
To gulp in lungfuls of diluted air
While others, papers raised, sneer to one side.

I long to put my feet up on the seat,
Ignoring muttered comments, looking bored,
And then without my heart missing one beat,
I'd flounce out confident I'd somehow scored.

Instead of which, with downcast eyes I sit,
Cough, shuffle on one buttock and that's it.

The Pool

Time is swimming in the same lane as me.
Lapping me, laughing at my leisurely, languorous crawl.
He churns up the water, rude rapid muscled butterfly.
He should move to the lane marked fast,
And get out of this one marked slow.
Now Time's pace slackens, I have him at my shoulder.
I am still crawling, lazily elegant,
But he has broken into breaststroke, cloying and contained,
And so we swim side by side, companionably.
I am suddenly breathless, but way out in front.
Time dog-paddles, inefficient, no kick at all.
I can't help winning.
I'll soon hit the wall.
I can't tumble turn.

The Dancing Lesson

Not unusual then that sullen boys
and girls would get the belt until the stroke
that brought the tears before the quiet class
and Eleanor the worst in every test
began to learn the hard way every week.
One day she tried to draw her hand away
and so he held her wrist to belt her more
and, caught, she jigged at every strike until
a whisper went from back to front, from top
to bottom of the class, *That's terrible.*
Our one rebellion lost. *And who wants more?*
We faced the front so only he would see
the eyes down in the lonely shame of fear
that we could be alone like Eleanor.

Papa

The talk was of how   he'd set out in the spring
once the ice had cleared   and his terror of snow
receded into its cave,   how he'd spear
the winter months   and cure them, save
the best of the apples,   prepare good lengths
of rope to keep   him safe whatever happened
then sit and speak with us   about his deep
love of the sea.
              And indeed light had just
begun to fill the room   and a faint white quality
of air to rise   like a thin glass dome
over the town   (though to us the ice
seemed solid still as stone)   the day he came down
and taking with him nothing   set out alone.

Unsinkable

Wife, husband, children all slide away
as the huge ship of their lust pulls out,
tickertape streaming down its sides, the quay
shrinking until they can hardly hear the shouts
and cries of well-wishers, the small
explosions shaking the town. They float on,
oblivious to reefs and shoals, the cruel
rocks that lurk just beneath the surface, borne
along a happiness so vast
they're convinced it must belong to everyone.
Below them, the holed wrecks of the past
subside slowly into memory, rust, bone.
They too were unsinkable, rigged for splendour,
foundered just beyond the harbour.

ALAN DUNNETT

Foxjaw

This man ran with a message as no other
man could until his heart stopped; this woman bound
kings with her beauty and wrote new laws, sometimes
in blood. These things took place long before you

and I were born in an ancient summer
with the jaws of foxes full of feathers
and fur in the growth of uncharted forests
and the last sabre-tooth crying for her mate.

Now you change with the times and take the train
to Brussels where you will trade on chocolate.
Back home, a jilted lover jogs round the park
while your new urban fox noses the bins,

overturns them, scoffs rubbish with ardour,
comfortable, unafraid, working to an end.

Catherine Edmunds

Advice

My mother said I shouldn't stay out late
and so I never did. Instead, I left
at dawn to turn a trick and meet my 'date',
thus pleasing Mum, who never knew the theft
of my virginity had been the task
of Uncle Percival; she never said
I shouldn't eat his sweets and mustn't ask
to see his winky when we were in bed.
My Mother taught me how to bake a cake
at gas mark 3, but buns in ovens weren't
a thing she mentioned. Bye-bye, my mistake,
aborted now, but still, at least I've learnt –
    for bad advice, there ain't nobody worse
    than stupid Mum and randy Uncle Perce.

Roadkill

A crow's huge baby, shiny, still and black,
Stranded in the road. Nowhere more alone
Than this. He stretches, conscious of his lack
Of strength, or skill, or future on his own.

The shape alarms me and I swerve and slow,
Missing him by inches. Ahead the road
Rolls on. I glance into the mirror, show
My concern, see the tiny life explode.

The car behind drives on, unseeing or
Just unperturbed. Too used, perhaps, to death
Like this, unheard, beneath the wheels, No more
Than tarmac space between us, one last breath.

For days, the carcase wing will lift as I
Drive past, as if in thanks, and make me cry.

The Destruction of Form

I'd nursed my son and put him down to sleep
then picked him up to feel his warmth once more,
a ritual I had come to love to keep
like clockwork on the hours: eight, twelve, and four.
My husband called. "Turn on TV," he said.
"Someone just fired on Kennedy's limousine."
I turned it on to hear Cronkite say: "He's dead,"
then took my son back to his crib and laid him down
in a new time without measured iambs
where life would stumble-dance along on two
left feet, all rhyme and reason gone,
where clocks like Dali's would slide down off the page,
their hands still trying to point to normal times
like poets trying to hold on to schemes with rhymes.

Diorama

Held for the shot, you swim against us, our torrent
of cuddling and babbling. Swim, wriggle and kick.
We would keep you as new as you are this instant
when we paste all futures on you and none stick.
Can there be any harm in these dioramas,
in hoping to fix your incipience forever?
You regard the chewable now, little Buddha,
undistracted by expectations; you've never
caught the sound of your voice and been afraid.
We clap blocks stacked and stacks dashed,
our work in progress, whose completion we dread,
whose every celebration is also a loss.
You arrive, take my hand and kiss your Mum
and tell us shyly who it is you've become.

Sundays

The last time you could scare me, you were swinging sods,
your handle long as me. What were we digging?
Soon these weekend chores would be done for good.
You didn't speak and I was sullen, roots jigging

my too-heavy spade, in the way of your blade's
quick sweep. You said: "Chop up kindling instead."
Out of sight of your lidded gaze, I sulked and played,
warily. Now you grip your stick, my arm. I lead

to those unbending Sundays a conversation
that shivers in the sunshine. You listen till I'm stuck.
This delving would appal those buried relations.
You look up: "I'm not proud of him." I'm shocked

by your dwindling. And scared of you again,
dug in to your shadow on the dazzling lawn.

Amalfi

You slept, skin slightly yellow, your eyes closed
So that I kissed your lids so gently, knowing
The little flutter gave you one quick smile
Before a sigh and a deeper sleep. You calm,
I crept out of the warmth of your sick smell
Slipped on my light night gown and stepped
Into the pearled grey dawn, stood at the view
Where the sea lay beyond the roof, just turning
In its sleep, awoken by that day's light touch.
Each morning I watched the sun turn up
The volume of the water, watched as one small
Boat came, night's work done, unhurried, taking
Its catch back across my view. It was
My morning prayer as I caught breath.

Holiday Snaps

Let me get one of you, with the church behind you.
She takes his 12 megapixel camera,
walks across St. Mark's Square. *She wants to fit*
the domes in too, he thinks. She strides through the arch

by Florian's. Continues up the Fondamenta
Orseolo, the Calle del Forno,
no-one remarking on this unremarkable woman
in comfortable sandals. Next up, the Ramo del Carbon:

past the little restaurant she hated
(leaving the camera on an outside table),
across the Rialto Bridge: hails a water-taxi,
shouts *Murano! Adriatico! Oceano!*

In the shadow of the Campanile, he wonders
how long he's got to clutch his slippery grin.

Finishing Touches

And so they stood on Castle Street,
Umbrellas dripping on their feet.
'Oh well,' she said. 'I'd better go.'
He nodded, stood unmoving, so
She leaned across and said that this
Could finish with a farewell kiss.

His lawyer stood and watched the pair,
The misty drizzle in their hair,
Which formed and fell in tiny drips,
While swift and fluently their lips,
Which knew each other's softest part,
Brushed lightly once; then drew apart.

'You're being very civilised,'
the lawyer said; unsure, surprised.

Robert Hamberger

Saying My Name

My mother doesn't know me from Adam.
She's baffled by my face, wonders at my words.
I make no sense; but if I tell her who I am
my name might echo down her corridors
to a room where she sits by open windows,
looking up from empty hands to find me there.
She'll hear Robert because of course she knows
those syllables, familiar as a prayer.
It's worth a shot. I say it like a stone
dropped into her lake to test the water,
to see if ripples bubble from my tone.
Nothing this time. I name my sons and daughter,
say her sisters' names, tell her all our news
to ease the silence, darkening like a bruise.

Twenty, Thirty Years Ago
(for Cliff)

No lullaby has ever occurred to me capable of singing him to rest.
                                        Virginia Woolf
                                        from *The Waves*

Talking tonight about his bitter death,
its pain, and how he hoped he'd never go,
where's the remedy? His name, that quick breath,
brings him back, standing by the window.
Once he said I was a brother to him.
Some people dance forever through your skin,
and twenty, thirty years ago we'd brim
with news, spilling our stories, two grown men
swapping language, gossiping like schoolgirls.
Once words ran out, we'd let ourselves be quiet,
as we stayed quiet for his drifts between pills
and sleep. I'd read to him, as I read his favourite
pages from *The Waves* when we were boys, believing
we'd ride against death, unvanquished, unyielding.

Untitled

We will never wake, tangled and smiling
together – nor look, half sleeping, with eyes
blinking slow depths into the beguiling
dawn – stretch, yawn, shed our sleep and exchange sighs.
We will never speak with silent, tender tongues
passion's plain language – never drink deep
love's intoxicating wine – satisfied, fill our lungs
with each other's breath – lie still – once more sleep.

We sit, animated by wine and light.
Our voices fight music, jostle with the crowd
in the last open bar; too full, too loud.
Poetry, the one passion that we share,
passes between us. I try not to care
too much, but wish I could hold you tonight.

On Balance

Like so many things in life, death comes and goes.
Last night, in dreaming, death slackened its grip
and you were there again, not bringing a message,
not struggling with something urgent: just there.

And when I'd woken you stayed awhile in memory,
smiling like the Cheshire Cat, until, out walking later,
I found an orange-red fox laid out on a lay-by's kerb:
pale-tipped tail still. Externally unbroken it seemed
simply to be forgetting, moment to moment, to breathe.

A spot of bright theatre blood spilt beside the jaw.
As if we'd met once, dead open eyes locked onto mine.

And I wondered whether this was the way that death
balanced his books: whether your one night back
could ever justify so still and such a senseless loss?

Optimisms

Both my old lovers are married now,
the two that counted, and not to me.
The knowledge of this settles slowly,
like snow at night. And as coldly.

It's like when the milk has turned
and the teaspoon penetrates deep
into a container containing no sugar
and yet the teabag's already in hot water.

The experience is exactly the same:
a small disappointment, slightly bitter.
Not enough to keep me awake at night.
Quite enough to keep me quiet.

And other things are disappointing too:
certain novels, some decisions. This.

First Thing

"I have studied the science of goodbyes."
                              Mandelstam (tr. Merwin/Brown)

I say goodbye to him each day I have
no early classes, stand here at the door
as he runs off to school, turns back to wave,
runs on, the hedge as it lifts hiding more
and more of him, and then there's just his hand
as he jumps thrusting it, until the bend,

and then back to my room and all this saved
up ink and paper time, and Tristia
in which, as Dante'd say, the sun's sweet rays
seem still to reach his eyes, and in his ears,
down through the empty coils, beyond all bounds:
the faint vibrations that had once been sounds,

such as a latch-click, cars passing, a boy's
feet running, all the data of goodbyes.

Disused Farm in Autumn

Out of a dismal sky a swallow dives,
circling fields where, once, tall bales of hay
stood stiff as soldiers. Leaves, like discarded lives,
collect in corners. Rain slants its grey
in puddles on the sodden land, patters
on broken windows. Deserted now, the farm
has only memories to unload. It scatters
them like seeds of grain from a careless palm.
An old barn door exhales a watery sigh,
admits its ghosts. The roof has almost gone.
Only the rafters remain to testify
to days of mirth and milking or what went on
in the loft on summer nights, lit by a June
sun or blessed by the silver scythe of the moon.

CHRISTOPHER JAMES

The Cat on the Dashboard

She sprawls on the dashboard like Marilyn,
across the hot, black lid of a Steinway.
This is how she likes it best, sunbathing
at ninety in the third lane, hypnotised
into slumber by a Saint Christopher, stretched
like a Persian rug; a slow sabre-toothed yawn.
Her owner sings at the wheel, wears Ray-Bans;
a phone lodged beneath her chin, courting
disaster, taking ten lives into her hands.
Not for them the cattery or travel cage;
the garden-gloved chase through the house:
this is a journey of mutual consent.
Ahead are the B-roads, the claws of trees
against the moon and cats eyes spilling with light.

Brick Work

Today, I'll dare to say:
We need to talk. I lean forward.
She does what she always does: shuts
her eyes, solid as walled-up windows.

To break in would be like raiding
a munitions store at night, in the dark
pulling pins out of hand grenades. For eighty years
she's kept her walls well pointed, cemented.

One small chink is all I'd need;
I'd find the most delicate chisel,
the softest brushes, work round the clock,
an archaeologist, coaxing one brick at a time.

She grabs the remote: *It's Countdown again.
Anyway, what time's your train?*

Editor's note: *Countdown* is a popular UK TV gameshow.

JULIE KANE

Used Book

What luck – an open bookstore up ahead
as rain lashed awnings over Royal Street,
and then to find the books were secondhand,
with one whole wall assigned to poetry;
and then, as if that wasn't luck enough,
to find, between Jarrell and Weldon Kees,
the blue-on-cream, familiar backbone of
my chapbook, out of print since '83 –
its cover very slightly coffee-stained,
but aging (all in all) no worse than flesh
through all those cycles of the seasons since
its publication by a London press.
Then, out of luck, I read the name inside:
the man I thought would love me till I died.

ROSEMARY J. KIND

The Fox Cub

A winter's tale of lengthened, darkened nights,
Of leafless, lifeless branches now laid bare,
Of fog that hangs on dank and frosty air,
Of northern, howling, bitter wind that bites.
A wounded fox cub, trapped still breathing fights,
To free his hind leg, bleeding, from the snare,
He longs for warmth and comfort of his lair,
Below the hillside's lofty, misty heights.

A quickened heart, when hearing footsteps tread,
Across the leaves from autumn, on the ground,
There stands a child, thank God, and not a man.
She bends to free him, tender strokes his head,
Takes off her sock and gently wraps it round,
His bleeding leg to mend it best she can.

Karen's Wedding

It takes a neighbour's marriage to bring out the best;
on the doorstep we're making the most of windy weather,
while Pom hands out anecdotes of weddings past,
like Murray-mints. "At least it's dry," we console one another,
sucking the sweets. Good measure, this waiting together.
Here's Karen's Dad, full-shouldered in the doorway,
unaccustomed and shiny as his crimson cravat, he never
imagined the heart-swelling terror of giving her away.
Here's Karen, photo-framed in the door-cheeks. Cameras sigh.

"Sometimes I lay awake a' neet," says Pom,
unwrapping the scene with his undertaker's eye
not quite retired from feet and inches, "and reckon
on t'houses in this street a've coffin'd, aye,
there's not many a one a've not coffin'd in my day."

Foot down

How they unwind themselves, these ropes
of roads: from slates to pantiles, apples
to olive oil, war graves to sailors' cliff-top
cemeteries. Tolls hurry us through forests
hung with black kites; mountains fade
into parallel horizons. After Clermont Ferrand
the rise is marked: five ... seven ... ten hundred metres
plus. In the down-slide, Norman Foster's miracle
stretches over Millau to the Grands Causses
flecked with close-cropped sheep. We squeeze
through blasted rock, hang over rivers, see tarmac
simmering and on the rush taste Fitou, Corbières.
My northern soul starts to unwrap its leaves –
a brussels sprout becoming a gardenia.

Keening

Afterwards, we sorted out his memory
In piles, some fast, some likely to run.
We laundered them and parcelled them on.
Dear Daddy, he loved us hard. Locking Mummy
In to keep the rapists out – to keep her intact.
And each time I left, words would become shards.
At the airport, his and my heart in shreds,
I would hug him and promise to come back.

I did return. On a beach, I see him,
A figure fixing his 'scope on the shoreline.
Seabirds wheel like cogs, their unoiled cries
A distant keening. There, we feel our loss.
Each visit recalls the grieving of the last.
Each visit, a gloss that ambers the past.

Christmas Truce

A Christmas chill stilettoes a winter morning,

while earth strains to its outer limit, the furthest
loop of its orbit, clearing the dirt for snow

to hack its thin flecks, for frost to curdle
in mud pools, still streaked with the blood of men,
and for wire to freeze to the touch of their fingers.

A head blinks from the lip of a parapet, unused
to the raw light, aching over hunched shoulders,
half-expecting the Maxim rattle, the shred
in his barking lungs, standing, by inches.

Others unfold around him, made bold
by his action, until a mob rubs hands
on clay, stretched with dismantled limbs,
listening hard, for the return of rolling guns.

Wrinkles

Yesterday I ironed your shirt and after I stroked
the creases out of the back, and uncrumpled
the arms from shoulder to wrist,
I slipped it on, with the collar still wrinkled.
It soothes my prickling skin while I wait for news.

When the baby cried and I held her,
she was quiet, her eyes half a shade darker
than my arms in your denim,
her cheek laid on the shoulder where mine loves to lie.

I'm ironing your plaid shirt now,
still wearing your denim.
It smells of milk and sweat
and the damp patch she's made.
I should wash it, but I'm warm and waiting…

Wartime Picnic

The gap in the hedge is thorny, but we're through,
sitting together in long rough grass, a bright
blessing of sunshine everywhere, and you
lying back, laughing, making it all feel right,
forgetting the bombs, your flags across the map,
our house half-full of strangers, and our man
somewhere unknown in Europe. You unwrap
tomatoes, bread – doing the best you can
with home-grown, queued-for, scarce; for me it's bliss
unbounded, the perfect day. Later I see
how brave you were that morning, and why this
is almost my only unstained memory
of you, of us. How soon it came about
that you stopped laughing, and the sun went out.

Romeo and Juliet for GCSE

I took my noisy class to the medlar tree
to look at some of Mercutio's "open arses".
The seasoned girls giggled knowingly
at the spread labia and tight five-pointed stars
but Lucy Chan picked two for her and me
and we held them in between our teeth like lovers
joined in a suicide pact. One, two, three!
We bit in unison and I laughed as her lips
puckered around unripened earthy sourness,
but Lucy mimed that I should chew and swallow
and when she arched a mock-quizzical eyebrow
I grinned collusively and mouthed "not really".
We'd started second bites down to the pips
before we heard the orchard's awkward silence.

Lessons

My darling, teach me how to love this bruise,
a swelling plum beneath my tautened skin.
The night's new fruit has grown in hours, contused
with rainbows. Show me, love, the beauty in
this loosened tooth, the rusty tang of blood,
its snag against my ripening lip – explain
the pleasure of this kick's adrenal flood,
the glory of the slap, the ministry of pain.
And curse me, sweetheart, spit, and educate
me in the ways of love with fists and fights,
the well-timed punch, the tender, delicate
last Glasgow kiss as you turn out my lights.
And, dear, by these lessons let me understand
this love, dealt by your soft, abusing hand.

Recipe

Passed down through women's hands, the book has found
its place with her, a pharmacopoeia
of love. To heal the sick, the cure-all blend
is chicken, carrots, schmaltz, some matzo flour
and patience. Time to simmer ancestry,
to rock her crying son and stroke his head.
The little room is thick with distant voices.
She tastes the fragrant broth and soothes the child,
remembers those who dug in Polish woods,
each cold and starved and flayed by memories
of wedding days and rosy motherhood,
the floured hands and magic alchemies
of gilded steamy kitchens, samovars
and aprons, hugs, the smell of a boy's hair.

The Mason's Art

Your profile, its pallor, hold me in awe.
You are chastened, like a knight on a tomb.
Hair slicked flat and secret eyes, you withdraw
from me. I shall lie next to you, assume
your calm. Across deep straits our elbows meet.
I am lust-clipped, penned in my pleated dress
and the small dog, who must be at our feet,
alert, like me, for your voice, shares the press
of silence. His crouched back is still, subdued
to our element – flesh, robes, plinth, all one.
My truant blood moves. You are stone-imbued,
sternly remade. Turn, say you are not gone
before me, you feel my warmth, this weight
of unsaid words, I have not come too late.

Muddles & Sparks

To the doctors, the scanners, his *corpus callosum*'s
dysmorphic, his fits a conforming event;
he can't walk or talk, control movement,
will never be Hawkin or Milton.
To Josh, elder brother, he's Matt.
Josh takes as he finds. Sees Matt fool the trap
with his humming, raised eyebrow, that grin.
Outside the trees shake. Leaves drift and swirl
as Josh pushes the buggy Matt's strapped in,
Dad hands him a leaf that says gold.
Back home Matt syringe-paints like Pollock,
is already, at three, his own man:
let the splodges and colours speak for him,
through his muddles and sparks shout *I can*.

André Mangeot

The Fabulists

Embarking, we are always dreamers. Odysseus
distracted all those years from Troy to Ithaca,
Dante's, Conrad's passage to the heart of darkness,
James T. Kirk advancing boldly on the future.
Now you and I upon *Minerva's* fore-deck, Chatwin
and Eberhardt perhaps, each eyeing the horizon
for our personal grail as we edge out from Valetta.
Tonight an eminent professor's due to talk on *Honour*
as a leitmotif in Ancient Greece; we have no better
guides to point the way, to bring all visible phenomena,
the voyage we shall make, to life. Nonetheless,
what journey, ever, failed to prove a deeper quest?
Embracing self-discovery, my love – hero or villain –
from here we are alone, our own Mercator and Magellan.

SUSANNE MATHIES

Flower Bed

Rabbits eat carnations, he explains,
You see some people never learn – it's cheap
but wasted. Sturdy fingers, marred by stains
from earth, tobacco and old age, digging deep
and pressing forth into the yielding mound,
searching, probing, plucking out a fare
of tangled roots. The stringy skeletons he found
cling to clumps of earth. He strips them bare.

A tidy square of orange mop heads nods
and points to nests of pansies, while he prods
a row of holes into the moist dark soil.
I ask him then. Which ones did she love best?
He stops, surprised. She never had them, lest
they make her sad. She worried they would spoil.

RICHARD MEIER

Raindrop/Teardrop

Keen to make us something, but unsure what,
I took a length of slender plywood, bent
it till its short sides touched, forming a point,
and joined them to each other. Then I cut
a base the shape of this thing's shape to slot
and fix inside it. Late that night I went
to your house bearing my experiment:
'Don't laugh,' I laughed, 'I'm not sure what I've got
here.' And when you stopped smirking and said, 'Well,
I love the raindrop/teardrop shape, but I'm
not sure, love, either,' there it was in words
what I could only put to you in wood:
'What is it we've been making all this time,
and will not tell?'

Unemployable

Neon hummed its grumbling light
through the cubicle.
The white scar of her parting
greeted him as she bent forward to write.
'Name and address? Age?'
He tried to remember, but couldn't quite,
watched her biro trap his guess onto the page.
'Occupation?'
She looked up, narrowed her eyes.
He moved his face closer to the glass divide.
'I am a healer of angels,' he replied.
'Look love, don't waste my time.'
Hands still in his pockets,
he ran one finger down the feather's spine.

DANIEL NEUMANN

Two Moments

Not wanting her to leave without a gift
(although in fact they'd never been to bed
or even close, in spite of what was said
by those who knew) he looked at earrings. Thrift
beset him when he saw the price: so tight
with Christmas coming up, and still to get
presents for Margaret and the children – yet
silver and turquoise gleamed against the light
and never would again. She's off to Perth
in seven days, it's a fine job, she'll go
and settle there and marry, never know
unless I give her these. The gesture's worth
a bit of scrape... Chance meeting, after years:
"Your husband gave me these," and touched her ears.

Belladonna Endings

Every day she waited in her garden
for roses and baby's breath to blossom,
but only the nightshades flourished,
threatening morning glory's hour.

Then a shock of relatives and friends gathered,
and at her doorstep caterers crowded each other,
packaging days in pre- and post-luncheons,
dinners lighted with toasts in her honor,
and of course the blessing of clerics.

Between the engagement and the wedding
came the florists,
between grief and the funeral, the musicians,
and in either case, what always remained was
red wine spilled on white damask.

The Revelation

I knew the anatomy of the shoulder;
how it worked on curves, the joint's smooth rig
and pulley – its elegant roll,
like Newton's boltless bridge.
I had focused on the eyes though,
or the places love can act;
looking for the perfect smile
like a curtain drawing back.
Perhaps it's simply that until your shoulders shone
last night when you wore that dress
that was a chalky halo draped around your chest,
their skin so young, a field unsown,
a God unphotographed, lost continents from lore –
I had never realised how beautiful your shoulders were
                                                    before.

Crucifix, Church of the Most Blessed Sacrament, Washington, D.C.

Stretched out in alabaster, now they see
this supple-muscled man. A plastercast display
of medieval pains fixed to a nave.
Blue wires and crumbled paint. It's lovely, in the way
cadavers sometimes are: vein-marbled arms
and bone-struck feet, the wincing simple face,
the painted hair. A thousand pricks of bees
adorn His flanks, and He adorns a star-filled space.

This starts you hating bodies all your life,
beginning with your own. In time you'll fault
the mirror's lively bursts, seeing this crime,
and shrink at last from touch, like snails from salt.

The beating heart drip-drops its doleful woes.
The children, filing past, go ones and twos.

WILLIAM OREM

News Item: Golden Retriever Abandoned in Field

In finding this, the breath inside you stops
like candlewick between wet fingers. See:
she's young, her black feet scabbed, all four legs wrapped
in tape. Her eyes have brewed two yellow leaks
to salve themselves. Around the snout rude blowflies
strut. Don't touch it, someone says, as if these
hurts have made her, too, unclean. But you must look –
you, having known the hands of men. Who feels
the life of other minds that share with us
this Earth? The injured hip the vet will find, the cuts
both old and fresh, beneath her coat; it's trust
undone, you know, that's worst. And so you sit

quite close to her, ashamed to be afraid.
The tail, with tiny hope, begins to sway.

Somewhere Else

Night and day you are the one,
only you beneath the moon...
but the residents in the lounge
where Home is somewhere else,
where the Sri Lankan staff try to be kind,
where the fish tank remains a mystery,
aren't listening to Sinatra's song.

Outside spring is beginning;
there's more yellow. A year ago,
stringing the earth in straight lines,
you sowed seeds ready for summer.
Now you prowl round brightly lit rooms,
search for something you can't remember
and stop to fathom the hinge of a door.

PAULINE PLUMMER

On Receiving a Disturbing Email

In a Northern town, lounging in leopard skin
a freckled woman of unfashionable size
who loves jokes, St. Francis and the seaside
thinks of her turbulent life. How to begin?
Sort through debris, photos of kids and kin,
prayers, sayings, bric-a-brac from other lives,
exotic hangings. They seem to advertise
several lives lived inside the same skin.

An email from a boyfriend of thirty years
ago flashbacks the girl who slept around
and valued fools' gold. It took grief and loss
to show what's real from what deceives.
The foolish ask why suffering's allowed.
Even a little wisdom comes at cost.

Wake

You've brisked off, leaving a slick of stubble,
a few drops of piss on the rim, some new
fingertip bruises on parts that won't trouble
the inquisitive, a smeared mirror, one or two
stains on the pillow, grit on the kitchen floor
and ten canes for a wigwam by the front door.

We've exchanged books, opinions, bodily fluids
cooked fish and potatoes, shaken a salad,
put ice in sherry, pepper on strawberries,
listened to the blackbird, watched videos,
strolled Paddy Lane and Spindle Wood,
searched the web for times of trains and ferries.

Your wake settles, the house rocks into balance.
The opposite of singing isn't silence.

Little Boy, Blue

I will not be remembered for my good works –
Christmases spent in soup kitchens,
charitable donations,
the giving of blood, marrow, a kidney.

Nor will the pages of the future
be remarkable for my contributions
to science, nature,
medicine, the arts.

Instead, my place in history,
my one small footnote in the journal of the world,
will be this single lapse:
Me asleep, my silent horn.
Some sheep in the meadow,
A cow in the corn.

Legendary Lover

Boys in the classroom
texted their love;

she felt the phone buzz,
an undertone

of constant passion
in her hip pocket,

too quiet
for Sir's ageing ears,

and she smiled, but chose
the one who took trouble

to write out in full
his worship, shape it

into a dart
and aim it home.

The Unconversations

He murmurs "Atkinson Terrace" or "Chinese crackers"
and she laughs softly, decoding at once
the shared references that baffle outsiders.

She will leave off halfway through a sentence;
he could finish it, if he felt the need.
Sometimes a gesture or a glance will do.

The longer the marriage, the more goes unsaid:
too much at stake for him to tell her now
that she cooks badly, that her snoring wakes him,

and she won't be mentioning her black tulip
missing from its bed, snapped off the stem
for a girl she cuts dead. Things to keep:

secrets, accounts, going, pretences up,
anything you've had a long time.

ANGELA READMAN

The Magician's Assistant

The magician's assistant in me is instantly stirred.
Improbable hair, sequin dress, I mirror-ball with a slow turn.
Here I am, just a nod, to make magic of hardboard props.
Your glance, no tricks, as I wave through an empty box,
and rabbits, I stopped naming, pop out like thoughts.
Another egg appears from bright paper cups;
I manage surprise. But you still look dashing in that old tux,
lead me though this routine we've danced so many times.
After, I brush droppings from your old hat, empty birds
from your pockets to inspect the wing-tipped shirt,
a sleeve, to find the flowers gone and only my heart.
I smile, as you slot the sword in and slide me apart;
a quick screen of smoke, the fountain of glitter I'm in,
someone else's toes wiggling.

A Wordsworthian Moment

The bridge's iron parapet was warm;
I leaned and watched the glittering river glide –
When all at once, beside my hand I spied
A crowd, a host, a company, a swarm
Of motile red dots, with eight whiskers
For legs; with aimless urgency each scurried
This way and that, unknowing why it hurried,
Sidestepping its swarming brothers and sisters.
Scarlet dots upon the black. Spiderlings.
In this corner of the universe, matter
Had formed itself into this living scatter –
These tiny, vivid, busy, fragile things.
So normal, yet so strange, what I was seeing:
Mysterious non-mystery of being.

Gynaecologist

If I had a lantern, no, a flaming pitch-tipped,
rag-wrapped torch, the skin's crystals
would shine as I felt my way deeper, slick
under foot. The light would flare over pools,
insinuate into cracks along the way,
till I offered it up to the undilated eye
of the cervix, the narrow strait
to the dark where life is stored and sired.
That's where I should be, riding the long tail
of a sperm, on and on, skirmishing, the thrill,
the race, the winning. I'd multiply, cell on cell,
becoming diverse, perfect, bubbling like spit.
When I withdraw from the muscular trumpet
my hand fits like a mute, what's left is an empty bell.

Ceremony

Stone by stone we levelled towards the sun
and still we are not safe: time's bailiffs waiting
beyond the walls are eager to begin
their own remorseless discipline of parting.

Absence like wind on water keeps no stillness.
I am not afraid of travelling further,
only of leaving with no word, no sweetness –
always one in this country, one in another.

Nothing can rescue love from death, but peace
may sometimes follow a pre-emptive strike.
Let us return to say our last goodbyes,
now, while the sun rides high, perform our wake:

our once and future affirmations heard,
we may deprive death of the final word.

Primer

I loved the feel of those grubby granular pages,
the intimate magic of the alphabet patterns;
would copy line by line, dipping my blunt split nib
in a white china well, blotting black teardrops.

I circled *a* for apple adding its little stalk
while *t* stood to *att*ention and *m*u*mm*y ran away.
The naughty nib splayed, blotching the letters
t for *t*rying, very *t*rying, *l* for *l*eft-handed, *l*azy.

Somehow I crossed the border to a country
where thought mysteriously scripted itself,
but shaping ideas onto waiting paper made me
afraid of having nothing important to say.

Now everything's joined-up, I've made my mark,
but I still dream of blotting my copy book.

JULIE-ANN ROWELL

On the Day I Didn't Know

The street was quiet on the day I didn't know,
pigeons went about their business along the windowsills,
the high street just as steep, the river on its way below,
the sun hidden, then re-emerging to soften the early chill.

On the day I didn't know, I dawdled on the hill –
I couldn't up the pace, lift myself, the usual shops
held no interest. Too much time to kill.
A busker sang a baleful tune, I did not stop

to hear his reason for the day. I reached the top
of town and found a place to buy a drink,
a compromise to help me home and swap
my dullness for reward, anything so as not to think.

On the day I didn't know, at home I locked the door.
I emptied dustbins, fed the cat, and mopped the floor.

First Days

shine always clearest: sunlight sharpening
blue geraniums on your muslin dress,
the firmness of your grip surprising me.
We laughed at napkins folded into swans,
the knives and spoons from different sets, the red
gondolas on the curtain. Back outside,
we paused; you smiled and walked towards your stop,
your head up high in sudden rain. I felt
the same as on my first Parisian day:
too keen, I lost myself in Châtelet's
high-ceilinged streets, where the bright neon arrows
and exit signs all led back to each other,
and I turned from shop to dizzy shop, unsure
of how to ask where I could find the sky.

DEREK SELLEN

Mother and Child

We were driving at thirty down Cambridge Hill
when, on a bike, her kid against the handle-bars,
this girl, not more than eighteen, grubby, small,
freewheeled through and shot the junction. The cars
went loco, swerving, hooting, brakes slammed hard,
but she just nervelessly looked back, one finger
in the air. The child whooped. She never veered,
arrow-straight for the next crossroads and its danger.

If they die, they'll die cheaply. A broom and bucket
will clear the tarmac of the feckless bitch and brat.
Better that, than leave us always on the look-out,
never knowing when they will pop up on the left or right
and send us into the path of a juggernaut head-on –
while they survive, riding on gravity through Armageddon.

Let Us Not Be Reconciled

So, we agreed to meet beneath our own carved oak
On the Common, in rain, its misty canopy
As good as gabled tile to the tensioning smoke
Of our cigarettes' embers, intermittently
Glowing and dim, as the harder we drew in breath
Like disbelief in silence going into one,
The more we knew each other as approaching death,
But clung on nonetheless, two lovers, with the sun

Behind them now, and nothing more ahead than ways
Our parents wreathed bouquets, raked over their living
Graves of hard-togetherness all week, just Sundays,
In slippers and dressing-gowns, mutually giving
Some glimpse of the mist long passed, immutable rain
On the windows and shutters, their racket of pain.

Sonnet on a One-Night Stand

His eyes were large and seaweed green, intense.
His voice was deep and gravelly, his hair
was spiked and brown. His biceps were immense
and tanned so that I couldn't wait to tear
the buttons from his shirt, and so we left
our drinks upon the sticky bar and got
a taxi to my flat. His tongue was deft
and warm, and more than once, it hit the spot

so I was disappointed when I woke,
to find a fat and balding man beneath
my sheets. I gagged and thought that I would choke
and searched the floor for a discarded sheath.
So my advice to you, it has to be
avoid the gin and stick to cups of tea!

The Mother to Their Son and Heir

You've got your father's chin, his mouth, his nose,
Your father's ease in well-heeled company,
The way he sparkles on the booze, that pose
He strikes, all winking affability.

You've got your father's charm, his downcast eyes,
The armfuls of apologies he brings
The morning after, the wan smile that buys
Another chance, mints clean new wedding rings.

I saw through her at once, the grasping bitch,
Laughing at the altar, thinking she'd won
A heart, an inheritance, not the rich
Rise, the stinging set of your father's sun.

You've got your father's chin. She's got my cheek,
My bruises, my lies, you his violent streak.

Chutney and War

While I undergo the process
of this unnecessary chore,
rescuing apples from bruised rot,
I wonder at the therapeutic ease
with which I breathe spice and sap.

I try to understand the slow,
deep stirring of molten autumn,
this urge to stash the harvest
into an unknown future,

and I feel very small dicing fruit
next to a radio blaring war.

I can only stir and bottle hope.

My proud jars stand in kitchen vaults,
wondering when he will be back.

CAROL A. TAYLOR

Legacy
(On the Death of a Friend's Mother)

I never knew you, yet I think the earth
must be somehow diminished by your death.
Your quiet garden blossomed with the birth
of seven splendid sons, your legacy.

I've lately wondered what God had in mind
to be my own bequest to humankind;
what challenge I've accepted or declined,
unwittingly fulfilling destiny.

The seeds of good and bad we sow on earth
take root before our passing; all the same,
we leave this world not knowing why we came

or whether generations down the line
some seed we planted, grown into a vine,
will prove to be the measure of our worth.

CHRISTINE TAYLOR

Coat

Her coat is made from closely woven twill,
chemical stink stitched into every seam.
Its lining is the North Sea's bitter chill
whose oily rainbow waters may deceive.

Her coat is so uncomfortable; it chafes.
She thinks she might suffocate, under mats
of rags, hand-me-downs, smog, dank, dismal places
and local lads their vowel sounds flat as caps.

If it takes her whole life, she'll shed this coat.
Bindings slashed by paper blades, refashioned.
Threads embroidered. The things she always loathed
unpicked. Then sewn again. Her own pattern.

But under satin, silk and crêpe de Chine,
she's still comforted to feel her gabardine.

Posthumous Instructions

After the fire, when I am rattling in my urn
and have no more to say to you, go home.
Have lunch. Ignore me, while I try to learn
the etiquette of ash and clinkerdom.

Let me settle. Let me reconcile
my boundaries with the cold geometry
of this strange vessel – my new domicile
whose curving contours reconfigure me.

Let me liberate the elements
that fused in me the morning I was formed
and offer them again, as evidence
that my short visit left the world unharmed.

My severance is what the world regains:
you do not need to scatter my remains.

Fullwoods End

Subversion of a name: you may be led
to picture foxglove strand and windmill sail.
No go: the truth's one more *Dunroamin'* vale
where, way ahead of fall, the trees twist dead.
A sunk place, linking Bilston's ancient grime
to tailbacks on the Birmingham New Road;
a raw park, station, pub: the neutral mode
of now, a tunnel for the gust of time.

Maybe. Yet schoolyears found me dragging through
its latticed ways at five. And that first date
secured me to its bus stop, to the view
of smoke and depot. Even now, though late
and speeding past, I brake, pull in and gaze
at all that curtained fastness, all my days.

After Rossnowlagh

Summer has darkened our street.
Privet sprouts bunches, and the climbing rose
has straggled almost halfway up the house.
In glutted gardens, fat apples bulge
like the bosoms of aunts in bathing suits.
On five sweet and heated afternoons,
under a mountainous approving sky,
in the sand-dunes of Donegal, a boy

kissed me. Now we shift our sights
to rites that send us, sleek, in our polished shoes
into the reek of the hedges' cut leaves
along familiar September routes.
In tight school uniform, in Latin class,
I whisper secrets I only half believe.

Ecstasy

I sit alone and wait, not for the bear exactly –
But to know what he may mean.

Tiny sounds bring great jolts of fear.
The maenads, in these dark groves, waiting for Dionysos,
Surely felt this same heady terror. Then they danced.
They danced, whirling and spinning until the whole world
Was diffused with golden light and they were dizzy,
Dazed with the truth that ecstasy imparts.

In the forest something splendid stirs,
My thudding heart feels it lurking there
Where fireflies flash and dazzle in the hollows.
I hear it padding over the leaf mould, coming closer,
Inexorably approaching. Not the bear, exactly,
But everything he means.

ELEANOR J. VALE

Journey

It was one of those stop start stop start journeys like when we were kids
and he took us to the beach and it took forever to do the fourteen miles.
It was one of those stop start stop start journeys
and the road works were everywhere like they always are in summer
and there were diversions and temporary lights
and single-line traffic holding us up all the time
and we were going to be late and the car was too hot
and we were sticky and sweaty and all dressed up.
The best thing about the journey
(because we weren't talking to each other like we usually do
and we didn't want to start remembering again)
so the best part was when we went past some workmen digging up the road
and one of them stopped and took off his hard hat and bowed his head
and he didn't even know my dad.

*Editor's note: this anthology is pocket-book sized and you will have seen that
ocasionally we have had to break a long line onto another using standard
conventions. With this sonnet, it seems a dreadful shame to do that and lose
the breathlessness; nor do we want to use smaller type. We have therefore
decided to print it as you see above.*

Junction 31

Airport Taxis

There may be a no smoking policy
but these Asian guys are usually ok?
All right if I smoke mate? Been a hell of a flight.
'No problem: been anywhere interesting?'
Kashmir, I tell him. He ponders a moment.
'Indian or Pakistan?' *Indian.*
'Aah…' We both fall silent and return.
I to the campfires, the saffron pickers
and the Floating Gardens of Srinagar.

He to the daily shelling, the terror,
confusion, loss and enforced separation.
On the road, always moving; even now,
each long mile, taking him further away.

It's Junction 31 mate. Almost home.

Sonnet on Slow Deaths

When I left I thought it would be easy
to forget the concrete floor, the nausea
of stale urine (it seems there are no ways
of abstracting it from stone), the shadow
of bars mocking in the sun. Even though
the creature was not on view one could sense,
in the hermetic existence, the slow
defeat; lost continents in the silence.

Would it have been worse if the animal
had emerged to prowl its soul about?
Thinking about it, I have to recall
Mr Price, life spent in bedridden state.

For forty years he lay there, without choice,
and each day dying; but, in his *own* place.

MALCOLM WATSON

Before the Fall

This perfect day, I see her reading in the green
Shade of the apple tree. Dappled sunlight strokes
Her hair, and flashes heliograms between the leaves.
Birds start to sing. And as I gaze, a million flowers
And I unfurl our hearts and what floods out is brighter
Than the sun. The warm breeze shakes the leaves
And weighs the swelling fruit. A few more weeks
Before they fall. If she should pluck for me that apple
Hanging from the tree, I'd give it back, not taste it. We
Would stay forever happy in this garden in the sun. She
Doesn't see the magpie flashing to the ground behind her,
But looks around and smiles at me when suddenly,
With perfect grace and timing, a second one appears.
And in this garden in the sun, all sorrow disappears.

Burnt

At ten past ten each day, the screens went up,
And then at ten-fifteen, the screams would start.
Thick bandages up to her chin had to be changed.
She was a mummy in a tragic mask. I was six
With a burst appendix. The screams would fade
To whimpers, but by then, I'd learnt to stop my ears.
A cloying antiseptic smell seeped from her bed
As she lay taut and panting, rolling her head.
She never smiled. How could I make her smile,
Just for a second, to take that agony away?
The day I left, I made her laugh by tripping up
And falling down as stupidly and gravely as a clown.
And every day since then I've seen that smile
And wished her balsam, spikenard and camomile.

JANE WEIR

A Dyer's Thoughts on Finding Scraps of Linen and Hessian, Wedged in Between Imported Goods

Down by the docks, waiting in the goods yard
for dyestuff, I'm aware of the presence
of tangerines, palm-stencilled dates, crates of Indian tea,
African coffee, mass-market blue and white plates,
stacked like Whitstable oysters, the air singed by spices.
I'm also aware, and these days increasingly so,
by what lies sandwiched between.
Rough cuts of natural hemp and linen sacking
that knowingly – like antiquity Gods – know
instinctively the ways of these goods.
Crumpled squares that soothe the rough,
leave well alone, keep well apart for the great distances.
Am I insane lingering on the humble cloth or does pure
thought grasp at the chance of a natural affinity?

EMRYS WESTACOTT

The Poet

She stands in a bedraggled solitude
at the garden's edge, overseeing combed soil
crusted with frost, her mouldy rags chewed
by weather and time, dutiful as a gargoyle.
There she stands, clothes-prop arms outstretched
in gratitude and grief, in happy shock
and hungry wonder at all the marvels fetched
by the given world – like this sudden flock
of words, blizzarding out of heavy skies
towards her, scoring the air with sweet alarms;
ten thousand bits of black scribble on the wing.
A few alight, peck her cheeks, peck her eyes,
jostle for perching rights on her head and arms,
arrange themselves along her frame, and sing.

MICHAEL J. WOODS

Early Doors

This was when to catch him in good spirits –
before the mid-evening rush and jostle,
before the calling for another bottle,
another pint, with hardly time to fill it.
Now he had the time to pass the time of day.
While the unwatched clock cut him some slack
he smoked, talked and joked as he topped up black,
patient porter. *Liffey water*, some would say.
Don knew better, ignored their ignorance
of the Wicklow mountain source. What is true
doesn't always go down well. Circumstance
dictates that knowledge benefits the few.
He set his clock – ten minutes ahead. Dead
on eleven he'd call time. Enough said.

Kathy Zwick

Treacherous History's Seeds

Pulsing autumn almonds – electric life,
Dicey recipe handed down to me,
Disks tossed by salty Baltic tidal strife,
Legacy of sad pines, sleeping history.

Orb-spider, fluffs of tattered feather,
Timid flecks of slanting northern sunshine,
Resin ovals strung along together,
Fossil chronicles chaptered in a line.

Murky forest of brute ox and tusked boar,
Delta battle fields, vicious hatreds sown,
Scenes of past loss on bleak Cretaceous shore.
What have these silent tears of resin known?

Poland's long treacherous history's seeds
Capsuled in my grandmother's cherished amber beads.

THE POETS

Mike Alexander lives in Houston, Texas. He is an administrator at the Sonnet Board, an on-line sonnet workshop. His idiosyncrasies include a devotion to the tenets of Symbolism & the employment of ampersands.

David Anthony is a British businessman and a Fellow of the Royal Society of Arts. His second poetry collection, *Talking to Lord Newborough*, was published in the USA by Alsop Review Press (2004). His work has appeared in various publications in North America, the UK and Japan.

Sharon Ashton was born in Birmingham in 1957, studied Latin and Classical Studies at Reading University and then trained as a nurse at St. Thomas' Hospital, London. She now lives in Shropshire, working part-time as a practice sister and studying part-time at Birmingham University for a BA in Creative Writing.

Polly Atkin was born in Nottingham, lived in London for seven years and now lives and works in Cumbria. She has recently had a poem commissioned by Arts Council England as part of their Abolition project. Her pamphlet *Bone Song* will be available from spring 2008.

Gill Baconnier was born in Cambridge in 1959, has won prizes for her poetry and has had short stories and articles published in various magazines. She is currently working on a children's novel. Gill is an English teacher in Grenoble, France, where she lives with her three teenage daughters.

Ginny Baily is a Devon-based writer whose stories and poetry have won awards, including the Plough Poetry Prize, and her work has been published in journals and anthologies, such as *Wasafiri* and *Momaya*. She founded and co-edits *Riptide*, a twice-yearly short story journal and is writing a novel set in Africa and Devon.

Richard Beban has been writing poetry since 1994. His poems in this volume are excerpted from a crown of sonnets. He lives in Playa del Rey, California, and Paris, France. More about him and his work can be found at www.beban.org.

Anna Bendix lives in South London, where she grew up. She has also lived in Brighton, Paris and Massachusetts. Her poems have recently been published in *Poetry News* and *Dream Catcher*.

Joan Benner grew up in East Anglia, but now lives in the Thames Valley. Born in 1925, and influenced by Eliot, Auden and MacNeice,

101

she was slow to find her own voice, but eventually minor prizes marked a breakthrough. Her work appears in various magazines and anthologies.

Adrian Blamires was born in Cornwall in 1964. He lives in Reading, Berkshire and teaches English in a sixth form college. He has published one collection of poems, *The Effect of Coastal Processes* (Two Rivers Press, 2005).

Peter Bloxsom is an Anglo-Australian freelance writer and website developer, living in Brisbane. His writing in various genres has been published over the past 30 years or so in the UK, Australia, and USA. He edits the sonnet webzine *14 by 14* (www.14by14.com) and co-edits *The Chimaera* (www.the-chimaera.com).

Ama Bolton is a gardener and book-artist, lives in Somerset and enjoys folk-dancing, motorcycling and spending time in pubs with fellow-poets.

Josephine Brogan is a Dundonian but has lived in Edinburgh for twenty years. These very different cities frame her mental landscape; she is always conscious of how much she owes them and her Scottish schooling. Josephine writes under her mother's name and to see it in a book form is very moving.

Alan Buckley was born in 1965 and brought up on Merseyside and now lives in Oxford. He has worked – among other things – as a forklift truck driver, a psychotherapist, and a poet in residence at a prison. His first pamphlet of poems is being published by tall-lighthouse in late 2008.

Brenda Ann Burke was born in Canada in 1959 and lives in Wellington, New Zealand. She has had work published in journals and anthologies and is currently collaborating on a collection, *The Smallest Lemon*, with artist Tristan Rodway. Apart from writing, Brenda's other life passion is training for endurance sport.

Chrissie Bury was born in Liverpool 1949. She trained as a teacher and enjoyed working in Finland, Bahrain and, later, Nepal. Married with two children and one grandchild, Chrissie lived and taught in Wiltshire and Cumbria, but is now resting in Yorkshire, writing, painting and making felt jewellery. She won the Kendal Ottaker's Poetry Prize in 2002.

Carol Caffrey hails from Ireland and lives in Shrewsbury with her husband and two teenage children. She has worked as a teacher and professional actress but is now a full-time writer. The poem in this anthology is dedicated to her late brother David, who introduced her to poetry and poets.

Carole Coates had her first collection, *The Goodbye Edition,* published in 2005 by Shoestring Press and Shoestring will publish her second in 2009. Her work appears regularly in the literary press and she has given many readings. She has also published critical writings. She lives in Lancaster.

Marina Collins was born in India, lived in Burma and educated in London. Among other things, she has taught English to adults, both here and abroad, worked in the Dome and been a legal proofreader. Although Marina has written little since her schooldays, this competition has prompted her to start again.

P. S. Cottier is an Australian poet based in Canberra, who escapes to the coast whenever possible. She wrote her PhD on animals in Dickens, and is also a qualified lawyer. She has recently begun to write full-time and has previously been published in Australia and the US.

Gordon Dargie was born in 1951 and brought up in Lanarkshire. A graduate of Glasgow University he taught English in Lanarkshire, Argyll and Shetland, where he recently retired as Principal of Shetland College and now feels he has the opportunity to write. He and his wife Maureen have two children.

Jane Draycott lives and works in Oxfordshire. Her previous collections include *Prince Rupert's Drop* and *The Night Tree* from Carcanet/Oxford, and *Tideway* (with images by Peter Hay) and *Christina the Astonishing* (co-written with Lesley Saunders), from Two Rivers Press.

Hugh Dunkerley has published two pamphlet collections, *Walking to the Fire Tower* (Redbeck Press) and *Fast* (Pighog Press). Individual poems have appeared in a variety of magazines and anthologies, including *Stand, The Fiddlehead* (Canada) and *Irish Pages*. A selection of his work recently featured in *Oxford Poets* 2007 (Carcanet).

Alan Dunnett was born London 1953, read English at Oxford and is currently Course Director of Drama Centre's MA Screen at Central Saint Martin's College of Art & Design. Alan's poems have appeared in magazines including *Stand, Pennine Platform, The Reader, The Rialto* and *Dream Catcher* and can be found at www.nthposition.com, www.shadowtrain.com and www.alandunnett.co.uk.

Catherine Edmunds worked for two decades as a classical musician before re-inventing herself as a writer and illustrator. Publications in 2008 include her solo poetry collection, *wormwood, earth and honey* (Circaidy Gregory Press), and illustrations for Daniel Abelman's *Allakazzam!* (BeWrite Books). Catherine lives in North-East England.

Amanda Ferguson was born in London in 1967. She lives in Oxfordshire with her husband and two daughters, working as a freelance copywriter. The Open Poetry Sonnet Competition entries were her first attempt at serious poetry for several years.

Gretchen Fletcher has found that poetry readings, awards and book signings have taken her from Ft. Lauderdale where she lives to San Francisco, Chicago, Kansas City, Boston, New York City, Dallas, and Houston. She publishes articles about her travels and leads writing workshops. Her chapbook, *That Severed Cord*, is to be published in June, 2008.

Alex Fox was born in Lincolnshire in 1974. He went to University in Leeds and lives there still, with his partner and two young sons. He works for a network of charities. Alex used to write for a rock climbing magazine. His poems have been published by *Agenda*.

Janice Fox has seen her short stories widely published; she won the Society of Authors' Tom-Gallon Award in 1997. Her work, as National Director of Care and Repair, was improving older people's housing conditions. Widowed with adult children, she campaigns on local health services in Nottingham, finding fulfilment in writing poetry.

Rosie Garland has three solo collections of poems and widely anthologised short stories and essays. Her first novel, *Animal Instinct*, is with her agent. She has an eclectic writing and performance history, from 80s Goth band 'The March Violets', to twisted cabaret as alter ego 'Rosie Lugosi the Vampire Queen'.

Judith Graham grew up in Perth, Western Australia and lived for over a decade in Germany. Sonnets have been an abiding pleasure for many years and she was previously runner-up in a *Sydney Morning Herald* sonnet competition. Judith now lives and works in central London.

Robert Hamberger has published five pamphlets, including the sonnet sequence *The Rule of Earth* (Smith/Doorstop, 2001) and *Heading North* (Flarestack, 2007). His full-length collections are *Warpaint Angel* (Blackwater Press, 1997), *The Smug Bridegroom* (Five Leaves, 2002) and *Torso* (Redbeck, 2007). He has been shortlisted for a Forward prize.

Oz Hardwick is a York-based writer and photographer. He has published two collections of poetry – *The Kind Ghosts* (Bluechrome, 2004) and *Carrying Fire* (Bluechrome, 2006) – as well as a book on medieval English comedy. He is Programme Leader in English and Writing at Leeds Trinity and All Saints.

A. F. Harrold is a writer and performer regularly seen on poetry and cabaret stages. *Logic and The Heart*, a collection of love poems, was published by Two Rivers Press in 2004. Two comic collections, *Postcards from the Hedgehog* and *The Man Who Spent Years in the Bath* are also available. See www.afharrold.co.uk.

John Haynes has published three books of poetry, the most recent of which, *Letter to Patience*, won the Costa Award for 2006. He lives in Hampshire with his Nigerian born wife and two children.

Doreen Hinchliffe was born in Yorkshire and now lives in London, where she teaches English as a Foreign Language. She started writing poetry twelve years ago and has won prizes or been commended in various competitions including the Petra Kenney and Peterloo. She is currently working on her first collection.

Christopher James has won the Bridport and Ledbury poetry prizes and is the recipient of an Eric Gregory Award from the Society of Authors. Born in Paisley, in 1975, he is also a graduate of the Creative Writing MA at the UEA. His first collection, *The Invention of Butterfly* (Ragged Raven, 2006), is available from www.raggedraven.co.uk

Pamela Johnson, novelist and poet, has published two novels, *Under Construction* and *Deep Blue Silence*, and her third, *Taking in Water*, received an Arts Council Writers' Award. Currently working on her first collection, her poems appear in anthologies. She lives in London and teaches on the MA in Creative Writing at Goldsmiths'.

Julie Kane is a native of Boston, Massachusetts, but has lived in Louisiana for more than three decades. She is an associate professor of English at Northwestern State University in Natchitoches, Louisiana. Her most recent poetry collection, *Rhythm & Booze* (2003), was a National Poetry Series winner and Poets' Prize finalist.

Rosemary Kind is a writer living in North Yorkshire. She writes a wide range of poems and stories for both adults and children. Her first volume of poems, *Poems For Life,* is available from www.poemsforlife.co.uk with all proceeds going to support the work of Age Concern in her home town of Leicestershire.

Sue Kindon shut the door on poetry when she left Hull, but failed to barricade it with sufficient heavy furniture so that, one day, when she was least expecting it, poetry burst back in on her. She currently lives in Cumbria.

Gill Learner is from Birmingham and now lives in Reading. Her poems have appeared in many anthologies and journals, including *Poetry News* and *Smiths Knoll*, and have won awards; she was shortlisted for the Keats-Shelley Prizes 2006 & 2007. She loves poetry workshops and reading at Reading's Poets' Café.

Gillian Livingstone was born in Northern Ireland in 1959. After receiving an MA from St Andrews University, she came to London to teach English. She now works with dyslexic students in higher and adult education. She has performed many of her poems, most recently a sonnet, written for her wedding.

Owen Lowery was born in Berkshire in 1968 and now lives near Liverpool which allows ample opportunity to explore long-standing historical, literary and sporting interests. Having recently completed an MA in Creative Writing at Bolton University, Owen is hoping to begin a related PhD in the not too distant future.

Sue Lozynskyj is encouraged in her writing by a lively network of writers across Yorkshire. She is published on the Poetry Society website, in many anthologies and the *Leeds Guide*. She has yet to publish a collection. Sue works as a midwife in East Yorkshire.

Alison Mace has written poems all her life, more freely since abandoning full-time teaching in 1988. She lives in Gloucestershire on the Welsh side of the Severn, has three adult daughters, and believes chronological age is irrelevant. She uses the sonnet form in this anthology to crystallise a real childhood memory.

Nick MacKinnon is a teacher at Winchester College, where there is an ancient medlar tree. His poems have appeared in *The New Statesman, Spectator, Warwick Review, Smiths Knoll* and *Anon*. He was a prize winner in the 2007 McLellan Festival.

Lydia Macpherson comes from Yorkshire. She now lives near Cambridge. She is reading for an MA in Creative Writing at Royal Holloway University of London. Her sonnet *Lessons* was first published in *The Warwick Review*. Other poems have appeared in various magazines, including *Poetry London* and *The Rialto*.

Anne Maney was born in Yorkshire in 1944. Her career has been in business, family, academic life, work with young people and teaching. Her writing has been persistent but reclusive. She lives in Clifford, near Leeds, and may be about to come out as a poet.

André Mangeot has two collections published to date: *Natural Causes* (Shoestring, 2003) and *Mixer* (Egg Box, 2005). He works for a charity in Cambridge and is also a member of the poetry performance group, 'The Joy of Six'. A book of short stories, *A Little Javanese* (Salt Publishing), is due in mid-2008.

Susanne Mathies lives in Zürich as an expatriate. She divides her time between business consulting, poetry and fiction writing, Open University studies, and reading anything that catches her fancy.

Richard Meier grew up in Surrey, then went to music school and university in Manchester. A selection of his poems appeared in

Carcanet's *Oxford Poets* anthology 2002. He now lives and works in London.

Eve Merkado grew up in South London and gained her BA in Fine Art from Rutgers University, USA. She has exhibited in Europe and the States. Eve lives in Hertfordshire where she teaches painting privately. She has recently turned her hand to poetry and this is her first publication.

Daniel Neumann was born in England in 1951 and has lived most of his life in Australia, where his poems have been published from time to time in various journals. He has two adult daughters and a granddaughter, and works as a classical musician and as a psychologist.

Phoebe Nilsen is Egyptian and was born in Zeitoun, Egypt, in 1949. She is also a Canadian citizen, is married to a Norwegian and has four adult children. At present, she is an associate professor at Nord-Trøndelag University College in central Norway, where she teaches ESL methodology and literature to teacher trainees.

Richard O'Brien was born in 1990. He is currently finishing A-levels and will soon, he hopes, be found in Brasenose College, Oxford, reading English and French. In 2006 and 2007 he was one of the 15 Foyle Young Poets of the Year. He is on the editorial team of *Pomegranate* e-zine.

William Orem has seen his short stories and poems appear in over 100 publications, including *The Princeton Arts Review, Alaska Quarterly Review, Sou'Wester* and *The New Formalist*, and he has been nominated for the Pushcart Prize in both genres. He is also a playwright, and currently works as Writer-In-Residence at Emerson College.

Geraldine Paine has been a professional actress, then a specialist teacher and writer. She gained an MPhil (Writing) from Glamorgan in 2000. Her poems have been published widely in magazines that include *The Rialto, THE SHOp* and *Agenda*. She was shortlisted for the Cinnamon Press Poetry Collection Competition, appearing in the 2007 anthology, *Shape Sifting*.

Pauline Plummer was born in Liverpool and lived in the North-East for 26 years. She has several collections of poetry published, including *Demon Straightening* (Iron Press, 2000), and short stories in collections. She tutors creative writing and has read her poetry on BBC Radio 4 and Tyne Tees TV. She has held residencies and taught writing in Sierra Leone, Ireland, France and Greece.

Patricia Pogson has published six collections of poetry. The latest, *Holding*, was issued by Flambard Press in 2002.

Andrew Proudfoot was born in Stevenage, in 1962 and currently works as a civil servant in Plymouth. His work has been previously published in anthologies by BeWrite and Happenstance Press and in *Poetry Nottingham*. He was runner-up in the 2005 Plough Prize (judge: Ian McMillan).

Sheenagh Pugh lives in Cardiff. She has published many collections of poems, two novels and a study of fan fiction. Her next collection, due out in autumn 2008 from Seren, will be called *Long-Haul Travellers* and contains several other sonnet variants, a form in which she's currently interested.

Angela Readman would love to include being a magician's assistant in her biography, but has mostly worked as a cleaner, painting houses, and teaching creative writing. Her collection *Strip* explores the world of porn stars through poetry (Salt Publishing, 2007.) She has had work published in *Ambit, Staple*, and in Frieda Hughes' column in *The Times*.

Brandon Robshaw was born in London in 1961. He is the author of several children's books including Puffin's *Tangshan Tigers* series. He lectures in literature and philosophy, and teaches creative writing for the Open University. He is a regular book reviewer for *The Independent on Sunday*. He is married with three children.

Sue Rose works as a literary translator. Her poetry has appeared in a variety of magazines and anthologies and she completed an MPhil in Writing at Glamorgan University under Gillian Clarke in 2004. Her first collection, *The Dark Room*, will be published by Bluechrome in October 2008.

Elisabeth Rowe read English at Somerville College, Oxford, taught English, raised a family, worked for the Citizens Advice Bureau service, and trained and worked as a social worker (childcare). She lives with her husband on Dartmoor and has three children and nine grandchildren. Her first collection, *Surface Tension,* was published by Peterloo Poets in 2003 and her second collection, *Thin Ice*, is due later 2008.

Julie-ann Rowell is a writer, editor and teacher. She has an MA in creative writing from Bath Spa University, and teaches part-time at Bristol University. Her pamphlet, *Convergence*, was a Poetry Book Society recommendation. Her first full collection is *Letters North,* published by Brodie Press.

Arun Sagar was born in 1982. He grew up in India, studied law, and is currently beginning a PhD in comparative federalism at Rouen University (Normandy). He has poems published or forthcoming in journals such as *Desilit Magazine, Soundzine* and *The Journal*.